BRIGHT LINE
MEAL PLANNER

WEIGHT LOSS EDITION

DATE: _____   WATER: ○ ○ ○ ○ ○ ○ ○ ○

MORNING GOALS:

BREAKFAST

1 PROTEIN:

1 GRAIN:

1 FRUIT:

LUNCH

1 PROTEIN:

6OZ VEGETABLE:

1 FRUIT:

1 FAT:

DINNER

1 PROTEIN:

6OZ VEGETABLE:

8OZ SALAD:

1 FAT:

DATE: _____   WATER: 💧💧💧💧💧💧💧💧

MORNING GOALS:

BREAKFAST	LUNCH	DINNER
1 PROTEIN:	1 PROTEIN:	1 PROTEIN:
1 GRAIN:	6OZ VEGETABLE:	6OZ VEGETABLE:
1 FRUIT:	1 FRUIT:	8OZ SALAD:
	1 FAT:	1 FAT:

DATE: _____ WATER: ○ ○ ○ ○ ○ ○ ○ ○

MORNING GOALS:

BREAKFAST

1 PROTEIN:

1 GRAIN:

1 FRUIT:

LUNCH

1 PROTEIN:

6OZ VEGETABLE:

1 FRUIT:

1 FAT:

DINNER

1 PROTEIN:

6OZ VEGETABLE:

8OZ SALAD:

1 FAT:

DATE: _____   WATER: ◇ ◇ ◇ ◇ ◇ ◇ ◇ ◇

MORNING GOALS:

BREAKFAST	LUNCH	DINNER
1 PROTEIN:	1 PROTEIN:	1 PROTEIN:
1 GRAIN:	6OZ VEGETABLE:	6OZ VEGETABLE:
1 FRUIT:	1 FRUIT:	8OZ SALAD:
	1 FAT:	1 FAT:

DATE: _____   WATER: ◊ ◊ ◊ ◊ ◊ ◊ ◊ ◊

MORNING GOALS:

BREAKFAST	LUNCH	DINNER
1 PROTEIN:	1 PROTEIN:	1 PROTEIN:
1 GRAIN:	6OZ VEGETABLE:	6OZ VEGETABLE:
1 FRUIT:	1 FRUIT:	8OZ SALAD:
	1 FAT:	1 FAT:

DATE: _____ WATER: 💧💧💧💧💧💧💧💧

MORNING GOALS:

BREAKFAST	LUNCH	DINNER
1 PROTEIN:	1 PROTEIN:	1 PROTEIN:
1 GRAIN:	6OZ VEGETABLE:	6OZ VEGETABLE:
1 FRUIT:	1 FRUIT:	8OZ SALAD:
	1 FAT:	1 FAT:

DATE: _____ WATER: ⬡ ⬡ ⬡ ⬡ ⬡ ⬡ ⬡ ⬡

MORNING GOALS:

BREAKFAST

1 PROTEIN:

1 GRAIN:

1 FRUIT:

LUNCH

1 PROTEIN:

6OZ VEGETABLE:

1 FRUIT:

1 FAT:

DINNER

1 PROTEIN:

6OZ VEGETABLE:

8OZ SALAD:

1 FAT:

DATE: _____ WATER: ⬯ ⬯ ⬯ ⬯ ⬯ ⬯ ⬯ ⬯

MORNING GOALS:

BREAKFAST	LUNCH	DINNER
1 PROTEIN:	1 PROTEIN:	1 PROTEIN:
1 GRAIN:	6OZ VEGETABLE:	6OZ VEGETABLE:
1 FRUIT:	1 FRUIT:	8OZ SALAD:
	1 FAT:	1 FAT:

DATE: _____   WATER: ○ ○ ○ ○ ○ ○ ○ ○

MORNING GOALS:

BREAKFAST

1 PROTEIN:

1 GRAIN:

1 FRUIT:

LUNCH

1 PROTEIN:

6OZ VEGETABLE:

1 FRUIT:

1 FAT:

DINNER

1 PROTEIN:

6OZ VEGETABLE:

8OZ SALAD:

1 FAT:

DATE: _____   WATER: 💧 💧 💧 💧 💧 💧 💧 💧

MORNING GOALS:

BREAKFAST	LUNCH	DINNER
1 PROTEIN:	1 PROTEIN:	1 PROTEIN:
1 GRAIN:	6OZ VEGETABLE:	6OZ VEGETABLE:
1 FRUIT:	1 FRUIT:	8OZ SALAD:
	1 FAT:	1 FAT:

DATE: _____ WATER: ○ ○ ○ ○ ○ ○ ○ ○

MORNING GOALS:

BREAKFAST

1 PROTEIN:

1 GRAIN:

1 FRUIT:

LUNCH

1 PROTEIN:

6OZ VEGETABLE:

1 FRUIT:

1 FAT:

DINNER

1 PROTEIN:

6OZ VEGETABLE:

8OZ SALAD:

1 FAT:

DATE: _____   WATER: 💧💧💧💧💧💧💧💧

MORNING GOALS:

BREAKFAST	LUNCH	DINNER
1 PROTEIN:	1 PROTEIN:	1 PROTEIN:
1 GRAIN:	6OZ VEGETABLE:	6OZ VEGETABLE:
1 FRUIT:	1 FRUIT:	8OZ SALAD:
	1 FAT:	1 FAT:

DATE: _____ WATER: 〇 〇 〇 〇 〇 〇 〇 〇

MORNING GOALS:

BREAKFAST

1 PROTEIN:

1 GRAIN:

1 FRUIT:

LUNCH

1 PROTEIN:

6OZ VEGETABLE:

1 FRUIT:

1 FAT:

DINNER

1 PROTEIN:

6OZ VEGETABLE:

8OZ SALAD:

1 FAT:

DATE: _____   WATER: 💧💧💧💧💧💧💧💧

MORNING GOALS:

BREAKFAST	LUNCH	DINNER
1 PROTEIN:	1 PROTEIN:	1 PROTEIN:
1 GRAIN:	6OZ VEGETABLE:	6OZ VEGETABLE:
1 FRUIT:	1 FRUIT:	8OZ SALAD:
	1 FAT:	1 FAT:

DATE: _____ WATER: ○ ○ ○ ○ ○ ○ ○ ○

MORNING GOALS:

BREAKFAST

1 PROTEIN:

1 GRAIN:

1 FRUIT:

LUNCH

1 PROTEIN:

6OZ VEGETABLE:

1 FRUIT:

1 FAT:

DINNER

1 PROTEIN:

6OZ VEGETABLE:

8OZ SALAD:

1 FAT:

DATE: _____   WATER: ○ ○ ○ ○ ○ ○ ○ ○

MORNING GOALS:

BREAKFAST	LUNCH	DINNER
1 PROTEIN:	1 PROTEIN:	1 PROTEIN:
1 GRAIN:	6OZ VEGETABLE:	6OZ VEGETABLE:
1 FRUIT:	1 FRUIT:	8OZ SALAD:
	1 FAT:	1 FAT:

DATE: _____ WATER: ○ ○ ○ ○ ○ ○ ○ ○

MORNING GOALS:

BREAKFAST

1 PROTEIN:

1 GRAIN:

1 FRUIT:

LUNCH

1 PROTEIN:

6OZ VEGETABLE:

1 FRUIT:

1 FAT:

DINNER

1 PROTEIN:

6OZ VEGETABLE:

8OZ SALAD:

1 FAT:

DATE: _____   WATER: ⚪ ⚪ ⚪ ⚪ ⚪ ⚪ ⚪ ⚪

MORNING GOALS:

BREAKFAST

1 PROTEIN:

1 GRAIN:

1 FRUIT:

LUNCH

1 PROTEIN:

6OZ VEGETABLE:

1 FRUIT:

1 FAT:

DINNER

1 PROTEIN:

6OZ VEGETABLE:

8OZ SALAD:

1 FAT:

DATE: _____   WATER: ○ ○ ○ ○ ○ ○ ○ ○

MORNING GOALS:

BREAKFAST

1 PROTEIN:

1 GRAIN:

1 FRUIT:

LUNCH

1 PROTEIN:

6OZ VEGETABLE:

1 FRUIT:

1 FAT:

DINNER

1 PROTEIN:

6OZ VEGETABLE:

8OZ SALAD:

1 FAT:

DATE: _____   WATER: ○ ○ ○ ○ ○ ○ ○ ○

MORNING GOALS:

BREAKFAST

1 PROTEIN:

1 GRAIN:

1 FRUIT:

LUNCH

1 PROTEIN:

6OZ VEGETABLE:

1 FRUIT:

1 FAT:

DINNER

1 PROTEIN:

6OZ VEGETABLE:

8OZ SALAD:

1 FAT:

DATE: _____   WATER: 💧💧💧💧💧💧💧💧

MORNING GOALS:

BREAKFAST

1 PROTEIN:

1 GRAIN:

1 FRUIT:

LUNCH

1 PROTEIN:

6OZ VEGETABLE:

1 FRUIT:

1 FAT:

DINNER

1 PROTEIN:

6OZ VEGETABLE:

8OZ SALAD:

1 FAT:

DATE: _____   WATER: ○ ○ ○ ○ ○ ○ ○ ○

MORNING GOALS:

BREAKFAST

1 PROTEIN:

1 GRAIN:

1 FRUIT:

LUNCH

1 PROTEIN:

6OZ VEGETABLE:

1 FRUIT:

1 FAT:

DINNER

1 PROTEIN:

6OZ VEGETABLE:

8OZ SALAD:

1 FAT:

DATE: _____   WATER: ○ ○ ○ ○ ○ ○ ○ ○

MORNING GOALS:

BREAKFAST

1 PROTEIN:

1 GRAIN:

1 FRUIT:

LUNCH

1 PROTEIN:

6OZ VEGETABLE:

1 FRUIT:

1 FAT:

DINNER

1 PROTEIN:

6OZ VEGETABLE:

8OZ SALAD:

1 FAT:

DATE: _____   WATER: 💧💧💧💧💧💧💧💧

MORNING GOALS:

BREAKFAST

1 PROTEIN:

1 GRAIN:

1 FRUIT:

LUNCH

1 PROTEIN:

6OZ VEGETABLE:

1 FRUIT:

1 FAT:

DINNER

1 PROTEIN:

6OZ VEGETABLE:

8OZ SALAD:

1 FAT:

DATE: _____ WATER: ◇ ◇ ◇ ◇ ◇ ◇ ◇ ◇

MORNING GOALS:

BREAKFAST	LUNCH	DINNER
1 PROTEIN:	1 PROTEIN:	1 PROTEIN:
1 GRAIN:	6OZ VEGETABLE:	6OZ VEGETABLE:
1 FRUIT:	1 FRUIT:	8OZ SALAD:
	1 FAT:	1 FAT:

DATE: _____ WATER: ○ ○ ○ ○ ○ ○ ○ ○

MORNING GOALS:

BREAKFAST

1 PROTEIN:

1 GRAIN:

1 FRUIT:

LUNCH

1 PROTEIN:

6OZ VEGETABLE:

1 FRUIT:

1 FAT:

DINNER

1 PROTEIN:

6OZ VEGETABLE:

8OZ SALAD:

1 FAT:

DATE: _____ WATER: ○ ○ ○ ○ ○ ○ ○ ○

MORNING GOALS:

BREAKFAST

1 PROTEIN:

1 GRAIN:

1 FRUIT:

LUNCH

1 PROTEIN:

6OZ VEGETABLE:

1 FRUIT:

1 FAT:

DINNER

1 PROTEIN:

6OZ VEGETABLE:

8OZ SALAD:

1 FAT:

DATE: _____   WATER: ○ ○ ○ ○ ○ ○ ○ ○

MORNING GOALS:

BREAKFAST

1 PROTEIN:

1 GRAIN:

1 FRUIT:

LUNCH

1 PROTEIN:

6OZ VEGETABLE:

1 FRUIT:

1 FAT:

DINNER

1 PROTEIN:

6OZ VEGETABLE:

8OZ SALAD:

1 FAT:

DATE: _____ WATER: ◯ ◯ ◯ ◯ ◯ ◯ ◯ ◯

MORNING GOALS:

BREAKFAST	LUNCH	DINNER
1 PROTEIN:	1 PROTEIN:	1 PROTEIN:
1 GRAIN:	6OZ VEGETABLE:	6OZ VEGETABLE:
1 FRUIT:	1 FRUIT:	8OZ SALAD:
	1 FAT:	1 FAT:

DATE: _____ WATER: ◊ ◊ ◊ ◊ ◊ ◊ ◊ ◊

MORNING GOALS:

BREAKFAST	LUNCH	DINNER
1 PROTEIN:	1 PROTEIN:	1 PROTEIN:
1 GRAIN:	6OZ VEGETABLE:	6OZ VEGETABLE:
1 FRUIT:	1 FRUIT:	8OZ SALAD:
	1 FAT:	1 FAT:

DATE: _____ WATER: ○ ○ ○ ○ ○ ○ ○ ○

MORNING GOALS:

BREAKFAST

1 PROTEIN:

1 GRAIN:

1 FRUIT:

LUNCH

1 PROTEIN:

6OZ VEGETABLE:

1 FRUIT:

1 FAT:

DINNER

1 PROTEIN:

6OZ VEGETABLE:

8OZ SALAD:

1 FAT:

DATE: _____ WATER: ◊ ◊ ◊ ◊ ◊ ◊ ◊ ◊

MORNING GOALS:

BREAKFAST

1 PROTEIN:

1 GRAIN:

1 FRUIT:

LUNCH

1 PROTEIN:

6OZ VEGETABLE:

1 FRUIT:

1 FAT:

DINNER

1 PROTEIN:

6OZ VEGETABLE:

8OZ SALAD:

1 FAT:

DATE: _____   WATER: ⬡ ⬡ ⬡ ⬡ ⬡ ⬡ ⬡ ⬡

MORNING GOALS:

BREAKFAST	LUNCH	DINNER
1 PROTEIN:	1 PROTEIN:	1 PROTEIN:
1 GRAIN:	6OZ VEGETABLE:	6OZ VEGETABLE:
1 FRUIT:	1 FRUIT:	8OZ SALAD:
	1 FAT:	1 FAT:

DATE: _____   WATER: ⚪⚪⚪⚪⚪⚪⚪⚪

MORNING GOALS:

BREAKFAST

1 PROTEIN:

1 GRAIN:

1 FRUIT:

LUNCH

1 PROTEIN:

6OZ VEGETABLE:

1 FRUIT:

1 FAT:

DINNER

1 PROTEIN:

6OZ VEGETABLE:

8OZ SALAD:

1 FAT:

DATE: _____ WATER: ○ ○ ○ ○ ○ ○ ○ ○

MORNING GOALS:

BREAKFAST

1 PROTEIN:

1 GRAIN:

1 FRUIT:

LUNCH

1 PROTEIN:

6OZ VEGETABLE:

1 FRUIT:

1 FAT:

DINNER

1 PROTEIN:

6OZ VEGETABLE:

8OZ SALAD:

1 FAT:

DATE: _____   WATER: ○ ○ ○ ○ ○ ○ ○ ○

MORNING GOALS:

BREAKFAST

1 PROTEIN:

1 GRAIN:

1 FRUIT:

LUNCH

1 PROTEIN:

6OZ VEGETABLE:

1 FRUIT:

1 FAT:

DINNER

1 PROTEIN:

6OZ VEGETABLE:

8OZ SALAD:

1 FAT:

DATE: _____ WATER: ○ ○ ○ ○ ○ ○ ○ ○

MORNING GOALS:

BREAKFAST

1 PROTEIN:

1 GRAIN:

1 FRUIT:

LUNCH

1 PROTEIN:

6OZ VEGETABLE:

1 FRUIT:

1 FAT:

DINNER

1 PROTEIN:

6OZ VEGETABLE:

8OZ SALAD:

1 FAT:

DATE: _____   WATER: ⚪ ⚪ ⚪ ⚪ ⚪ ⚪ ⚪ ⚪

MORNING GOALS:

BREAKFAST	LUNCH	DINNER
1 PROTEIN:	1 PROTEIN:	1 PROTEIN:
1 GRAIN:	6OZ VEGETABLE:	6OZ VEGETABLE:
1 FRUIT:	1 FRUIT:	8OZ SALAD:
	1 FAT:	1 FAT:

DATE: _____

WATER: ⚪ ⚪ ⚪ ⚪ ⚪ ⚪ ⚪ ⚪

MORNING GOALS:

BREAKFAST

1 PROTEIN:

1 GRAIN:

1 FRUIT:

LUNCH

1 PROTEIN:

6OZ VEGETABLE:

1 FRUIT:

1 FAT:

DINNER

1 PROTEIN:

6OZ VEGETABLE:

8OZ SALAD:

1 FAT:

DATE: _____   WATER: ◯ ◯ ◯ ◯ ◯ ◯ ◯ ◯

MORNING GOALS:

BREAKFAST	LUNCH	DINNER
1 PROTEIN:	1 PROTEIN:	1 PROTEIN:
1 GRAIN:	6OZ VEGETABLE:	6OZ VEGETABLE:
1 FRUIT:	1 FRUIT:	8OZ SALAD:
	1 FAT:	1 FAT:

DATE: _____ WATER: ○ ○ ○ ○ ○ ○ ○ ○

MORNING GOALS:

BREAKFAST	LUNCH	DINNER
1 PROTEIN:	1 PROTEIN:	1 PROTEIN:
1 GRAIN:	6OZ VEGETABLE:	6OZ VEGETABLE:
1 FRUIT:	1 FRUIT:	8OZ SALAD:
	1 FAT:	1 FAT:

DATE: _____ WATER: ○ ○ ○ ○ ○ ○ ○ ○

MORNING GOALS:

BREAKFAST

1 PROTEIN:

1 GRAIN:

1 FRUIT:

LUNCH

1 PROTEIN:

6OZ VEGETABLE:

1 FRUIT:

1 FAT:

DINNER

1 PROTEIN:

6OZ VEGETABLE:

8OZ SALAD:

1 FAT:

DATE: _____   WATER: ◯ ◯ ◯ ◯ ◯ ◯ ◯ ◯

MORNING GOALS:

BREAKFAST

1 PROTEIN:

1 GRAIN:

1 FRUIT:

LUNCH

1 PROTEIN:

6OZ VEGETABLE:

1 FRUIT:

1 FAT:

DINNER

1 PROTEIN:

6OZ VEGETABLE:

8OZ SALAD:

1 FAT:

DATE: _____   WATER: 💧💧💧💧💧💧💧💧

MORNING GOALS:

BREAKFAST

1 PROTEIN:

1 GRAIN:

1 FRUIT:

LUNCH

1 PROTEIN:

6OZ VEGETABLE:

1 FRUIT:

1 FAT:

DINNER

1 PROTEIN:

6OZ VEGETABLE:

8OZ SALAD:

1 FAT:

DATE: _____ WATER: ◌ ◌ ◌ ◌ ◌ ◌ ◌ ◌

MORNING GOALS:

BREAKFAST	LUNCH	DINNER
1 PROTEIN:	1 PROTEIN:	1 PROTEIN:
1 GRAIN:	6OZ VEGETABLE:	6OZ VEGETABLE:
1 FRUIT:	1 FRUIT:	8OZ SALAD:
	1 FAT:	1 FAT:

DATE: _____   WATER: ⬭ ⬭ ⬭ ⬭ ⬭ ⬭ ⬭ ⬭

MORNING GOALS:

BREAKFAST	LUNCH	DINNER
1 PROTEIN:	1 PROTEIN:	1 PROTEIN:
1 GRAIN:	6OZ VEGETABLE:	6OZ VEGETABLE:
1 FRUIT:	1 FRUIT:	8OZ SALAD:
	1 FAT:	1 FAT:

DATE: _____   WATER: 💧💧💧💧💧💧💧💧

MORNING GOALS:

BREAKFAST

1 PROTEIN:

1 GRAIN:

1 FRUIT:

LUNCH

1 PROTEIN:

6OZ VEGETABLE:

1 FRUIT:

1 FAT:

DINNER

1 PROTEIN:

6OZ VEGETABLE:

8OZ SALAD:

1 FAT:

DATE: _____   WATER: ⬡ ⬡ ⬡ ⬡ ⬡ ⬡ ⬡ ⬡

MORNING GOALS:

BREAKFAST	LUNCH	DINNER
1 PROTEIN:	1 PROTEIN:	1 PROTEIN:
1 GRAIN:	6OZ VEGETABLE:	6OZ VEGETABLE:
1 FRUIT:	1 FRUIT:	8OZ SALAD:
	1 FAT:	1 FAT:

DATE: _____ WATER: ◯ ◯ ◯ ◯ ◯ ◯ ◯ ◯

MORNING GOALS:

BREAKFAST	LUNCH	DINNER
1 PROTEIN:	1 PROTEIN:	1 PROTEIN:
1 GRAIN:	6OZ VEGETABLE:	6OZ VEGETABLE:
1 FRUIT:	1 FRUIT:	8OZ SALAD:
	1 FAT:	1 FAT:

DATE: _____   WATER: 🜄 🜄 🜄 🜄 🜄 🜄 🜄 🜄

MORNING GOALS:

BREAKFAST	LUNCH	DINNER
1 PROTEIN:	1 PROTEIN:	1 PROTEIN:
1 GRAIN:	6OZ VEGETABLE:	6OZ VEGETABLE:
1 FRUIT:	1 FRUIT:	8OZ SALAD:
	1 FAT:	1 FAT:

DATE: _____   WATER: ⬭ ⬭ ⬭ ⬭ ⬭ ⬭ ⬭ ⬭

MORNING GOALS:

BREAKFAST

1 PROTEIN:

1 GRAIN:

1 FRUIT:

LUNCH

1 PROTEIN:

6OZ VEGETABLE:

1 FRUIT:

1 FAT:

DINNER

1 PROTEIN:

6OZ VEGETABLE:

8OZ SALAD:

1 FAT:

DATE: _____ WATER: ○ ○ ○ ○ ○ ○ ○ ○

MORNING GOALS:

BREAKFAST

1 PROTEIN:

1 GRAIN:

1 FRUIT:

LUNCH

1 PROTEIN:

6OZ VEGETABLE:

1 FRUIT:

1 FAT:

DINNER

1 PROTEIN:

6OZ VEGETABLE:

8OZ SALAD:

1 FAT:

DATE: _____   WATER: ⬭ ⬭ ⬭ ⬭ ⬭ ⬭ ⬭ ⬭

MORNING GOALS:

BREAKFAST	LUNCH	DINNER
1 PROTEIN:	1 PROTEIN:	1 PROTEIN:
1 GRAIN:	6OZ VEGETABLE:	6OZ VEGETABLE:
1 FRUIT:	1 FRUIT:	8OZ SALAD:
	1 FAT:	1 FAT:

DATE: _____   WATER: ○ ○ ○ ○ ○ ○ ○ ○

MORNING GOALS:

BREAKFAST

1 PROTEIN:

1 GRAIN:

1 FRUIT:

LUNCH

1 PROTEIN:

6OZ VEGETABLE:

1 FRUIT:

1 FAT:

DINNER

1 PROTEIN:

6OZ VEGETABLE:

8OZ SALAD:

1 FAT:

DATE: _____   WATER: ◊ ◊ ◊ ◊ ◊ ◊ ◊ ◊

MORNING GOALS:

BREAKFAST	LUNCH	DINNER
1 PROTEIN:	1 PROTEIN:	1 PROTEIN:
1 GRAIN:	6OZ VEGETABLE:	6OZ VEGETABLE:
1 FRUIT:	1 FRUIT:	8OZ SALAD:
	1 FAT:	1 FAT:

DATE: _____   WATER: ◊ ◊ ◊ ◊ ◊ ◊ ◊ ◊

MORNING GOALS:

BREAKFAST

1 PROTEIN:

1 GRAIN:

1 FRUIT:

LUNCH

1 PROTEIN:

6OZ VEGETABLE:

1 FRUIT:

1 FAT:

DINNER

1 PROTEIN:

6OZ VEGETABLE:

8OZ SALAD:

1 FAT:

DATE: _____ WATER: ⬭ ⬭ ⬭ ⬭ ⬭ ⬭ ⬭

MORNING GOALS:

BREAKFAST

1 PROTEIN:

1 GRAIN:

1 FRUIT:

LUNCH

1 PROTEIN:

6OZ VEGETABLE:

1 FRUIT:

1 FAT:

DINNER

1 PROTEIN:

6OZ VEGETABLE:

8OZ SALAD:

1 FAT:

DATE: _____ WATER: ○ ○ ○ ○ ○ ○ ○ ○

MORNING GOALS:

BREAKFAST	LUNCH	DINNER
1 PROTEIN:	1 PROTEIN:	1 PROTEIN:
1 GRAIN:	6OZ VEGETABLE:	6OZ VEGETABLE:
1 FRUIT:	1 FRUIT:	8OZ SALAD:
	1 FAT:	1 FAT:

DATE: _____ WATER: ○ ○ ○ ○ ○ ○ ○ ○

MORNING GOALS:

BREAKFAST

1 PROTEIN:

1 GRAIN:

1 FRUIT:

LUNCH

1 PROTEIN:

6OZ VEGETABLE:

1 FRUIT:

1 FAT:

DINNER

1 PROTEIN:

6OZ VEGETABLE:

8OZ SALAD:

1 FAT:

DATE: _____   WATER: ○ ○ ○ ○ ○ ○ ○ ○

MORNING GOALS:

BREAKFAST

1 PROTEIN:

1 GRAIN:

1 FRUIT:

LUNCH

1 PROTEIN:

6OZ VEGETABLE:

1 FRUIT:

1 FAT:

DINNER

1 PROTEIN:

6OZ VEGETABLE:

8OZ SALAD:

1 FAT:

DATE: _____   WATER: 💧💧💧💧💧💧💧💧

MORNING GOALS:

BREAKFAST

1 PROTEIN:

1 GRAIN:

1 FRUIT:

LUNCH

1 PROTEIN:

6OZ VEGETABLE:

1 FRUIT:

1 FAT:

DINNER

1 PROTEIN:

6OZ VEGETABLE:

8OZ SALAD:

1 FAT:

DATE: _____   WATER: ○ ○ ○ ○ ○ ○ ○ ○

MORNING GOALS:

BREAKFAST

1 PROTEIN:

1 GRAIN:

1 FRUIT:

LUNCH

1 PROTEIN:

6OZ VEGETABLE:

1 FRUIT:

1 FAT:

DINNER

1 PROTEIN:

6OZ VEGETABLE:

8OZ SALAD:

1 FAT:

DATE: _____   WATER: ○ ○ ○ ○ ○ ○ ○ ○

MORNING GOALS:

BREAKFAST

1 PROTEIN:

1 GRAIN:

1 FRUIT:

LUNCH

1 PROTEIN:

6OZ VEGETABLE:

1 FRUIT:

1 FAT:

DINNER

1 PROTEIN:

6OZ VEGETABLE:

8OZ SALAD:

1 FAT:

DATE: _____   WATER: ◊ ◊ ◊ ◊ ◊ ◊ ◊ ◊

MORNING GOALS:

BREAKFAST	LUNCH	DINNER
1 PROTEIN:	1 PROTEIN:	1 PROTEIN:
1 GRAIN:	6OZ VEGETABLE:	6OZ VEGETABLE:
1 FRUIT:	1 FRUIT:	8OZ SALAD:
	1 FAT:	1 FAT:

DATE: _____   WATER: ○ ○ ○ ○ ○ ○ ○ ○

MORNING GOALS:

BREAKFAST	LUNCH	DINNER
1 PROTEIN:	1 PROTEIN:	1 PROTEIN:
1 GRAIN:	6OZ VEGETABLE:	6OZ VEGETABLE:
1 FRUIT:	1 FRUIT:	8OZ SALAD:
	1 FAT:	1 FAT:

DATE: _____   WATER: 💧💧💧💧💧💧💧💧

MORNING GOALS:

BREAKFAST	LUNCH	DINNER
1 PROTEIN:	1 PROTEIN:	1 PROTEIN:
1 GRAIN:	6OZ VEGETABLE:	6OZ VEGETABLE:
1 FRUIT:	1 FRUIT:	8OZ SALAD:
	1 FAT:	1 FAT:

DATE: _____   WATER: 💧 💧 💧 💧 💧 💧 💧 💧

MORNING GOALS:

BREAKFAST

1 PROTEIN:

1 GRAIN:

1 FRUIT:

LUNCH

1 PROTEIN:

6OZ VEGETABLE:

1 FRUIT:

1 FAT:

DINNER

1 PROTEIN:

6OZ VEGETABLE:

8OZ SALAD:

1 FAT:

DATE: _____   WATER: ○ ○ ○ ○ ○ ○ ○ ○

MORNING GOALS:

BREAKFAST

1 PROTEIN:

1 GRAIN:

1 FRUIT:

LUNCH

1 PROTEIN:

6OZ VEGETABLE:

1 FRUIT:

1 FAT:

DINNER

1 PROTEIN:

6OZ VEGETABLE:

8OZ SALAD:

1 FAT:

DATE: _____   WATER: ◊ ◊ ◊ ◊ ◊ ◊ ◊ ◊

MORNING GOALS:

BREAKFAST

1 PROTEIN:

1 GRAIN:

1 FRUIT:

LUNCH

1 PROTEIN:

6OZ VEGETABLE:

1 FRUIT:

1 FAT:

DINNER

1 PROTEIN:

6OZ VEGETABLE:

8OZ SALAD:

1 FAT:

DATE: _____   WATER: 💧 💧 💧 💧 💧 💧 💧 💧

MORNING GOALS:

BREAKFAST	LUNCH	DINNER
1 PROTEIN:	1 PROTEIN:	1 PROTEIN:
1 GRAIN:	6OZ VEGETABLE:	6OZ VEGETABLE:
1 FRUIT:	1 FRUIT:	8OZ SALAD:
	1 FAT:	1 FAT:

DATE: _____   WATER: ○ ○ ○ ○ ○ ○ ○ ○

MORNING GOALS:

BREAKFAST

1 PROTEIN:

1 GRAIN:

1 FRUIT:

LUNCH

1 PROTEIN:

6OZ VEGETABLE:

1 FRUIT:

1 FAT:

DINNER

1 PROTEIN:

6OZ VEGETABLE:

8OZ SALAD:

1 FAT:

DATE: _____ WATER: ◇ ◇ ◇ ◇ ◇ ◇ ◇ ◇

MORNING GOALS:

BREAKFAST

1 PROTEIN:

1 GRAIN:

1 FRUIT:

LUNCH

1 PROTEIN:

6OZ VEGETABLE:

1 FRUIT:

1 FAT:

DINNER

1 PROTEIN:

6OZ VEGETABLE:

8OZ SALAD:

1 FAT:

DATE: _____   WATER: ○ ○ ○ ○ ○ ○ ○ ○

MORNING GOALS:

BREAKFAST

1 PROTEIN:

1 GRAIN:

1 FRUIT:

LUNCH

1 PROTEIN:

6OZ VEGETABLE:

1 FRUIT:

1 FAT:

DINNER

1 PROTEIN:

6OZ VEGETABLE:

8OZ SALAD:

1 FAT:

DATE: _____	WATER: ○ ○ ○ ○ ○ ○ ○ ○

MORNING GOALS:

BREAKFAST	LUNCH	DINNER
1 PROTEIN:	1 PROTEIN:	1 PROTEIN:
1 GRAIN:	6OZ VEGETABLE:	6OZ VEGETABLE:
1 FRUIT:	1 FRUIT:	8OZ SALAD:
	1 FAT:	1 FAT:

DATE: _____   WATER: ○ ○ ○ ○ ○ ○ ○ ○

MORNING GOALS:

BREAKFAST

1 PROTEIN:

1 GRAIN:

1 FRUIT:

LUNCH

1 PROTEIN:

6OZ VEGETABLE:

1 FRUIT:

1 FAT:

DINNER

1 PROTEIN:

6OZ VEGETABLE:

8OZ SALAD:

1 FAT:

DATE: _____ WATER: ○ ○ ○ ○ ○ ○ ○ ○

MORNING GOALS:

BREAKFAST	LUNCH	DINNER
1 PROTEIN:	1 PROTEIN:	1 PROTEIN:
1 GRAIN:	6OZ VEGETABLE:	6OZ VEGETABLE:
1 FRUIT:	1 FRUIT:	8OZ SALAD:
	1 FAT:	1 FAT:

DATE: _____   WATER: ○ ○ ○ ○ ○ ○ ○ ○

MORNING GOALS:

BREAKFAST

1 PROTEIN:

1 GRAIN:

1 FRUIT:

LUNCH

1 PROTEIN:

6OZ VEGETABLE:

1 FRUIT:

1 FAT:

DINNER

1 PROTEIN:

6OZ VEGETABLE:

8OZ SALAD:

1 FAT:

DATE: _____   WATER: 💧💧💧💧💧💧💧💧

MORNING GOALS:

BREAKFAST	LUNCH	DINNER
1 PROTEIN:	1 PROTEIN:	1 PROTEIN:
1 GRAIN:	6OZ VEGETABLE:	6OZ VEGETABLE:
1 FRUIT:	1 FRUIT:	8OZ SALAD:
	1 FAT:	1 FAT:

DATE: _____ WATER: ○ ○ ○ ○ ○ ○ ○ ○

MORNING GOALS:

BREAKFAST

1 PROTEIN:

1 GRAIN:

1 FRUIT:

LUNCH

1 PROTEIN:

6OZ VEGETABLE:

1 FRUIT:

1 FAT:

DINNER

1 PROTEIN:

6OZ VEGETABLE:

8OZ SALAD:

1 FAT:

DATE: _____

WATER: ◊ ◊ ◊ ◊ ◊ ◊ ◊ ◊

MORNING GOALS:

BREAKFAST

1 PROTEIN:

1 GRAIN:

1 FRUIT:

LUNCH

1 PROTEIN:

6OZ VEGETABLE:

1 FRUIT:

1 FAT:

DINNER

1 PROTEIN:

6OZ VEGETABLE:

8OZ SALAD:

1 FAT:

DATE: _____ WATER: ○ ○ ○ ○ ○ ○ ○ ○

MORNING GOALS:

BREAKFAST

1 PROTEIN:

1 GRAIN:

1 FRUIT:

LUNCH

1 PROTEIN:

6OZ VEGETABLE:

1 FRUIT:

1 FAT:

DINNER

1 PROTEIN:

6OZ VEGETABLE:

8OZ SALAD:

1 FAT:

DATE: _____ WATER: ○ ○ ○ ○ ○ ○ ○ ○

MORNING GOALS:

BREAKFAST

1 PROTEIN:

1 GRAIN:

1 FRUIT:

LUNCH

1 PROTEIN:

6OZ VEGETABLE:

1 FRUIT:

1 FAT:

DINNER

1 PROTEIN:

6OZ VEGETABLE:

8OZ SALAD:

1 FAT:

DATE: _____   WATER: ⚪ ⚪ ⚪ ⚪ ⚪ ⚪ ⚪ ⚪

MORNING GOALS:

BREAKFAST	LUNCH	DINNER
1 PROTEIN:	1 PROTEIN:	1 PROTEIN:
1 GRAIN:	6OZ VEGETABLE:	6OZ VEGETABLE:
1 FRUIT:	1 FRUIT:	8OZ SALAD:
	1 FAT:	1 FAT:

DATE: _____ WATER: ◊ ◊ ◊ ◊ ◊ ◊ ◊ ◊

MORNING GOALS:

BREAKFAST	LUNCH	DINNER
1 PROTEIN:	1 PROTEIN:	1 PROTEIN:
1 GRAIN:	6OZ VEGETABLE:	6OZ VEGETABLE:
1 FRUIT:	1 FRUIT:	8OZ SALAD:
	1 FAT:	1 FAT:

DATE: _____   WATER: ○ ○ ○ ○ ○ ○ ○ ○

MORNING GOALS:

BREAKFAST

1 PROTEIN:

1 GRAIN:

1 FRUIT:

LUNCH

1 PROTEIN:

6OZ VEGETABLE:

1 FRUIT:

1 FAT:

DINNER

1 PROTEIN:

6OZ VEGETABLE:

8OZ SALAD:

1 FAT:

DATE: _____   WATER: ○ ○ ○ ○ ○ ○ ○ ○

MORNING GOALS:

BREAKFAST	LUNCH	DINNER
1 PROTEIN:	1 PROTEIN:	1 PROTEIN:
1 GRAIN:	6OZ VEGETABLE:	6OZ VEGETABLE:
1 FRUIT:	1 FRUIT:	8OZ SALAD:
	1 FAT:	1 FAT:

DATE: _____   WATER: 💧 💧 💧 💧 💧 💧 💧 💧

MORNING GOALS:

BREAKFAST

1 PROTEIN:

1 GRAIN:

1 FRUIT:

LUNCH

1 PROTEIN:

6OZ VEGETABLE:

1 FRUIT:

1 FAT:

DINNER

1 PROTEIN:

6OZ VEGETABLE:

8OZ SALAD:

1 FAT:

DATE: _____   WATER: ○ ○ ○ ○ ○ ○ ○ ○

MORNING GOALS:

BREAKFAST

1 PROTEIN:

1 GRAIN:

1 FRUIT:

LUNCH

1 PROTEIN:

6OZ VEGETABLE:

1 FRUIT:

1 FAT:

DINNER

1 PROTEIN:

6OZ VEGETABLE:

8OZ SALAD:

1 FAT:

DATE: _____   WATER: ○ ○ ○ ○ ○ ○ ○ ○

MORNING GOALS:

BREAKFAST

1 PROTEIN:

1 GRAIN:

1 FRUIT:

LUNCH

1 PROTEIN:

6OZ VEGETABLE:

1 FRUIT:

1 FAT:

DINNER

1 PROTEIN:

6OZ VEGETABLE:

8OZ SALAD:

1 FAT:

DATE: _____   WATER: ◇ ◇ ◇ ◇ ◇ ◇ ◇ ◇

MORNING GOALS:

BREAKFAST	LUNCH	DINNER
1 PROTEIN:	1 PROTEIN:	1 PROTEIN:
1 GRAIN:	6OZ VEGETABLE:	6OZ VEGETABLE:
1 FRUIT:	1 FRUIT:	8OZ SALAD:
	1 FAT:	1 FAT:

DATE: _____   WATER: ◊ ◊ ◊ ◊ ◊ ◊ ◊ ◊

MORNING GOALS:

BREAKFAST

1 PROTEIN:

1 GRAIN:

1 FRUIT:

LUNCH

1 PROTEIN:

6OZ VEGETABLE:

1 FRUIT:

1 FAT:

DINNER

1 PROTEIN:

6OZ VEGETABLE:

8OZ SALAD:

1 FAT:

DATE: _____ WATER: ○ ○ ○ ○ ○ ○ ○ ○

MORNING GOALS:

BREAKFAST

1 PROTEIN:

1 GRAIN:

1 FRUIT:

LUNCH

1 PROTEIN:

6OZ VEGETABLE:

1 FRUIT:

1 FAT:

DINNER

1 PROTEIN:

6OZ VEGETABLE:

8OZ SALAD:

1 FAT:

DATE: _____ WATER: ◯ ◯ ◯ ◯ ◯ ◯ ◯ ◯

MORNING GOALS:

BREAKFAST

1 PROTEIN:

1 GRAIN:

1 FRUIT:

LUNCH

1 PROTEIN:

6OZ VEGETABLE:

1 FRUIT:

1 FAT:

DINNER

1 PROTEIN:

6OZ VEGETABLE:

8OZ SALAD:

1 FAT:

DATE: _____   WATER: ◯ ◯ ◯ ◯ ◯ ◯ ◯ ◯

MORNING GOALS:

BREAKFAST	LUNCH	DINNER
1 PROTEIN:	1 PROTEIN:	1 PROTEIN:
1 GRAIN:	6OZ VEGETABLE:	6OZ VEGETABLE:
1 FRUIT:	1 FRUIT:	8OZ SALAD:
	1 FAT:	1 FAT:

DATE: _____ WATER: ⬡ ⬡ ⬡ ⬡ ⬡ ⬡ ⬡ ⬡

MORNING GOALS:

BREAKFAST	LUNCH	DINNER
1 PROTEIN:	1 PROTEIN:	1 PROTEIN:
1 GRAIN:	6OZ VEGETABLE:	6OZ VEGETABLE:
1 FRUIT:	1 FRUIT:	8OZ SALAD:
	1 FAT:	1 FAT:

DATE: _____ WATER: ◯ ◯ ◯ ◯ ◯ ◯ ◯ ◯

MORNING GOALS:

BREAKFAST

1 PROTEIN:

1 GRAIN:

1 FRUIT:

LUNCH

1 PROTEIN:

6OZ VEGETABLE:

1 FRUIT:

1 FAT:

DINNER

1 PROTEIN:

6OZ VEGETABLE:

8OZ SALAD:

1 FAT:

DATE: _____ WATER: ○ ○ ○ ○ ○ ○ ○ ○

MORNING GOALS:

BREAKFAST

1 PROTEIN:

1 GRAIN:

1 FRUIT:

LUNCH

1 PROTEIN:

6OZ VEGETABLE:

1 FRUIT:

1 FAT:

DINNER

1 PROTEIN:

6OZ VEGETABLE:

8OZ SALAD:

1 FAT:

DATE: _____   WATER: 💧💧💧💧💧💧💧💧

MORNING GOALS:

BREAKFAST

1 PROTEIN:

1 GRAIN:

1 FRUIT:

LUNCH

1 PROTEIN:

6OZ VEGETABLE:

1 FRUIT:

1 FAT:

DINNER

1 PROTEIN:

6OZ VEGETABLE:

8OZ SALAD:

1 FAT:

DATE: _____ WATER: ○ ○ ○ ○ ○ ○ ○ ○

MORNING GOALS:

BREAKFAST

1 PROTEIN:

1 GRAIN:

1 FRUIT:

LUNCH

1 PROTEIN:

6OZ VEGETABLE:

1 FRUIT:

1 FAT:

DINNER

1 PROTEIN:

6OZ VEGETABLE:

8OZ SALAD:

1 FAT:

DATE: _____   WATER: ○ ○ ○ ○ ○ ○ ○ ○

MORNING GOALS:

BREAKFAST

1 PROTEIN:

1 GRAIN:

1 FRUIT:

LUNCH

1 PROTEIN:

6OZ VEGETABLE:

1 FRUIT:

1 FAT:

DINNER

1 PROTEIN:

6OZ VEGETABLE:

8OZ SALAD:

1 FAT:

DATE: _____   WATER: ⚪⚪⚪⚪⚪⚪⚪⚪

MORNING GOALS:

BREAKFAST

1 PROTEIN:

1 GRAIN:

1 FRUIT:

LUNCH

1 PROTEIN:

6OZ VEGETABLE:

1 FRUIT:

1 FAT:

DINNER

1 PROTEIN:

6OZ VEGETABLE:

8OZ SALAD:

1 FAT:

DATE: _____ WATER: ◊ ◊ ◊ ◊ ◊ ◊ ◊ ◊

MORNING GOALS:

BREAKFAST

1 PROTEIN:

1 GRAIN:

1 FRUIT:

LUNCH

1 PROTEIN:

6OZ VEGETABLE:

1 FRUIT:

1 FAT:

DINNER

1 PROTEIN:

6OZ VEGETABLE:

8OZ SALAD:

1 FAT:

DATE: _____   WATER: 💧💧💧💧💧💧💧💧

MORNING GOALS:

BREAKFAST

1 PROTEIN:

1 GRAIN:

1 FRUIT:

LUNCH

1 PROTEIN:

6OZ VEGETABLE:

1 FRUIT:

1 FAT:

DINNER

1 PROTEIN:

6OZ VEGETABLE:

8OZ SALAD:

1 FAT:

DATE: _____ WATER: ○ ○ ○ ○ ○ ○ ○ ○

MORNING GOALS:

BREAKFAST	LUNCH	DINNER
1 PROTEIN:	1 PROTEIN:	1 PROTEIN:
1 GRAIN:	6OZ VEGETABLE:	6OZ VEGETABLE:
1 FRUIT:	1 FRUIT:	8OZ SALAD:
	1 FAT:	1 FAT:

DATE: _____   WATER: 💧💧💧💧💧💧💧

MORNING GOALS:

BREAKFAST

1 PROTEIN:

1 GRAIN:

1 FRUIT:

LUNCH

1 PROTEIN:

6OZ VEGETABLE:

1 FRUIT:

1 FAT:

DINNER

1 PROTEIN:

6OZ VEGETABLE:

8OZ SALAD:

1 FAT:

DATE: _____   WATER: ○ ○ ○ ○ ○ ○ ○ ○

MORNING GOALS:

BREAKFAST

1 PROTEIN:

1 GRAIN:

1 FRUIT:

LUNCH

1 PROTEIN:

6OZ VEGETABLE:

1 FRUIT:

1 FAT:

DINNER

1 PROTEIN:

6OZ VEGETABLE:

8OZ SALAD:

1 FAT:

DATE: _____   WATER: ○ ○ ○ ○ ○ ○ ○ ○

MORNING GOALS:

BREAKFAST

1 PROTEIN:

1 GRAIN:

1 FRUIT:

LUNCH

1 PROTEIN:

6OZ VEGETABLE:

1 FRUIT:

1 FAT:

DINNER

1 PROTEIN:

6OZ VEGETABLE:

8OZ SALAD:

1 FAT:

DATE: _____   WATER: ○ ○ ○ ○ ○ ○ ○ ○

MORNING GOALS:

BREAKFAST

1 PROTEIN:

1 GRAIN:

1 FRUIT:

LUNCH

1 PROTEIN:

6OZ VEGETABLE:

1 FRUIT:

1 FAT:

DINNER

1 PROTEIN:

6OZ VEGETABLE:

8OZ SALAD:

1 FAT:

DATE: _____ WATER: ○ ○ ○ ○ ○ ○ ○ ○

MORNING GOALS:

BREAKFAST

1 PROTEIN:

1 GRAIN:

1 FRUIT:

LUNCH

1 PROTEIN:

6OZ VEGETABLE:

1 FRUIT:

1 FAT:

DINNER

1 PROTEIN:

6OZ VEGETABLE:

8OZ SALAD:

1 FAT:

DATE: _____   WATER: 💧💧💧💧💧💧💧💧

MORNING GOALS:

BREAKFAST	LUNCH	DINNER
1 PROTEIN:	1 PROTEIN:	1 PROTEIN:
1 GRAIN:	6OZ VEGETABLE:	6OZ VEGETABLE:
1 FRUIT:	1 FRUIT:	8OZ SALAD:
	1 FAT:	1 FAT:

DATE: _____   WATER: ○ ○ ○ ○ ○ ○ ○ ○

MORNING GOALS:

BREAKFAST

1 PROTEIN:

1 GRAIN:

1 FRUIT:

LUNCH

1 PROTEIN:

6OZ VEGETABLE:

1 FRUIT:

1 FAT:

DINNER

1 PROTEIN:

6OZ VEGETABLE:

8OZ SALAD:

1 FAT:

DATE: _____   WATER: ○ ○ ○ ○ ○ ○ ○ ○

MORNING GOALS:

BREAKFAST	LUNCH	DINNER
1 PROTEIN:	1 PROTEIN:	1 PROTEIN:
1 GRAIN:	6OZ VEGETABLE:	6OZ VEGETABLE:
1 FRUIT:	1 FRUIT:	8OZ SALAD:
	1 FAT:	1 FAT:

DATE: _____ WATER: ○ ○ ○ ○ ○ ○ ○ ○

MORNING GOALS:

BREAKFAST

1 PROTEIN:

1 GRAIN:

1 FRUIT:

LUNCH

1 PROTEIN:

6OZ VEGETABLE:

1 FRUIT:

1 FAT:

DINNER

1 PROTEIN:

6OZ VEGETABLE:

8OZ SALAD:

1 FAT:

DATE: _____   WATER: 💧💧💧💧💧💧💧

MORNING GOALS:

BREAKFAST	LUNCH	DINNER
1 PROTEIN:	1 PROTEIN:	1 PROTEIN:
1 GRAIN:	6OZ VEGETABLE:	6OZ VEGETABLE:
1 FRUIT:	1 FRUIT:	8OZ SALAD:
	1 FAT:	1 FAT:

DATE: _____   WATER: 💧💧💧💧💧💧💧💧

MORNING GOALS:

BREAKFAST

1 PROTEIN:

1 GRAIN:

1 FRUIT:

LUNCH

1 PROTEIN:

6OZ VEGETABLE:

1 FRUIT:

1 FAT:

DINNER

1 PROTEIN:

6OZ VEGETABLE:

8OZ SALAD:

1 FAT:

DATE: _____   WATER: ◊ ◊ ◊ ◊ ◊ ◊ ◊ ◊

MORNING GOALS:

BREAKFAST	LUNCH	DINNER
1 PROTEIN:	1 PROTEIN:	1 PROTEIN:
1 GRAIN:	6OZ VEGETABLE:	6OZ VEGETABLE:
1 FRUIT:	1 FRUIT:	8OZ SALAD:
	1 FAT:	1 FAT:

DATE: _____   WATER: ○ ○ ○ ○ ○ ○ ○ ○

MORNING GOALS:

BREAKFAST

1 PROTEIN:

1 GRAIN:

1 FRUIT:

LUNCH

1 PROTEIN:

6OZ VEGETABLE:

1 FRUIT:

1 FAT:

DINNER

1 PROTEIN:

6OZ VEGETABLE:

8OZ SALAD:

1 FAT:

DATE: _____   WATER: ○ ○ ○ ○ ○ ○ ○ ○

MORNING GOALS:

BREAKFAST

1 PROTEIN:

1 GRAIN:

1 FRUIT:

LUNCH

1 PROTEIN:

6OZ VEGETABLE:

1 FRUIT:

1 FAT:

DINNER

1 PROTEIN:

6OZ VEGETABLE:

8OZ SALAD:

1 FAT:

DATE: _____   WATER: ○ ○ ○ ○ ○ ○ ○ ○

MORNING GOALS:

BREAKFAST

1 PROTEIN:

1 GRAIN:

1 FRUIT:

LUNCH

1 PROTEIN:

6OZ VEGETABLE:

1 FRUIT:

1 FAT:

DINNER

1 PROTEIN:

6OZ VEGETABLE:

8OZ SALAD:

1 FAT:

DATE: _____ WATER: ○ ○ ○ ○ ○ ○ ○ ○

MORNING GOALS:

BREAKFAST

1 PROTEIN:

1 GRAIN:

1 FRUIT:

LUNCH

1 PROTEIN:

6OZ VEGETABLE:

1 FRUIT:

1 FAT:

DINNER

1 PROTEIN:

6OZ VEGETABLE:

8OZ SALAD:

1 FAT:

DATE: _____ WATER: ○ ○ ○ ○ ○ ○ ○ ○

MORNING GOALS:

BREAKFAST

1 PROTEIN:

1 GRAIN:

1 FRUIT:

LUNCH

1 PROTEIN:

6OZ VEGETABLE:

1 FRUIT:

1 FAT:

DINNER

1 PROTEIN:

6OZ VEGETABLE:

8OZ SALAD:

1 FAT:

DATE: _____ WATER: ◯ ◯ ◯ ◯ ◯ ◯ ◯ ◯

MORNING GOALS:

BREAKFAST	LUNCH	DINNER
1 PROTEIN:	1 PROTEIN:	1 PROTEIN:
1 GRAIN:	6OZ VEGETABLE:	6OZ VEGETABLE:
1 FRUIT:	1 FRUIT:	8OZ SALAD:
	1 FAT:	1 FAT:

DATE: _____   WATER: 💧💧💧💧💧💧💧💧

MORNING GOALS:

BREAKFAST	LUNCH	DINNER
1 PROTEIN:	1 PROTEIN:	1 PROTEIN:
1 GRAIN:	6OZ VEGETABLE:	6OZ VEGETABLE:
1 FRUIT:	1 FRUIT:	8OZ SALAD:
	1 FAT:	1 FAT:

DATE: _____   WATER: ○ ○ ○ ○ ○ ○ ○ ○

MORNING GOALS:

BREAKFAST

1 PROTEIN:

1 GRAIN:

1 FRUIT:

LUNCH

1 PROTEIN:

6OZ VEGETABLE:

1 FRUIT:

1 FAT:

DINNER

1 PROTEIN:

6OZ VEGETABLE:

8OZ SALAD:

1 FAT:

DATE: _____ WATER: 💧💧💧💧💧💧💧💧

MORNING GOALS:

BREAKFAST

1 PROTEIN:

1 GRAIN:

1 FRUIT:

LUNCH

1 PROTEIN:

6OZ VEGETABLE:

1 FRUIT:

1 FAT:

DINNER

1 PROTEIN:

6OZ VEGETABLE:

8OZ SALAD:

1 FAT:

DATE: _____ WATER: ○ ○ ○ ○ ○ ○ ○ ○

MORNING GOALS:

BREAKFAST

1 PROTEIN:

1 GRAIN:

1 FRUIT:

LUNCH

1 PROTEIN:

6OZ VEGETABLE:

1 FRUIT:

1 FAT:

DINNER

1 PROTEIN:

6OZ VEGETABLE:

8OZ SALAD:

1 FAT:

DATE: _____   WATER: 💧💧💧💧💧💧💧💧

MORNING GOALS:

BREAKFAST

1 PROTEIN:

1 GRAIN:

1 FRUIT:

LUNCH

1 PROTEIN:

6OZ VEGETABLE:

1 FRUIT:

1 FAT:

DINNER

1 PROTEIN:

6OZ VEGETABLE:

8OZ SALAD:

1 FAT:

DATE: _____   WATER: ○ ○ ○ ○ ○ ○ ○ ○

MORNING GOALS:

BREAKFAST

1 PROTEIN:

1 GRAIN:

1 FRUIT:

LUNCH

1 PROTEIN:

6OZ VEGETABLE:

1 FRUIT:

1 FAT:

DINNER

1 PROTEIN:

6OZ VEGETABLE:

8OZ SALAD:

1 FAT:

DATE: _____ WATER: ◯ ◯ ◯ ◯ ◯ ◯ ◯ ◯

MORNING GOALS:

BREAKFAST

1 PROTEIN:

1 GRAIN:

1 FRUIT:

LUNCH

1 PROTEIN:

6OZ VEGETABLE:

1 FRUIT:

1 FAT:

DINNER

1 PROTEIN:

6OZ VEGETABLE:

8OZ SALAD:

1 FAT:

DATE: _____   WATER: ○ ○ ○ ○ ○ ○ ○ ○

MORNING GOALS:

BREAKFAST	LUNCH	DINNER
1 PROTEIN:	1 PROTEIN:	1 PROTEIN:
1 GRAIN:	6OZ VEGETABLE:	6OZ VEGETABLE:
1 FRUIT:	1 FRUIT:	8OZ SALAD:
	1 FAT:	1 FAT:

DATE: _____   WATER: ○ ○ ○ ○ ○ ○ ○ ○

MORNING GOALS:

BREAKFAST

1 PROTEIN:

1 GRAIN:

1 FRUIT:

LUNCH

1 PROTEIN:

6OZ VEGETABLE:

1 FRUIT:

1 FAT:

DINNER

1 PROTEIN:

6OZ VEGETABLE:

8OZ SALAD:

1 FAT:

DATE: _____ WATER: ◊ ◊ ◊ ◊ ◊ ◊ ◊ ◊

MORNING GOALS:

BREAKFAST	LUNCH	DINNER
1 PROTEIN:	1 PROTEIN:	1 PROTEIN:
1 GRAIN:	6OZ VEGETABLE:	6OZ VEGETABLE:
1 FRUIT:	1 FRUIT:	8OZ SALAD:
	1 FAT:	1 FAT:

DATE: _____   WATER: ◯ ◯ ◯ ◯ ◯ ◯ ◯ ◯

MORNING GOALS:

BREAKFAST

1 PROTEIN:

1 GRAIN:

1 FRUIT:

LUNCH

1 PROTEIN:

6OZ VEGETABLE:

1 FRUIT:

1 FAT:

DINNER

1 PROTEIN:

6OZ VEGETABLE:

8OZ SALAD:

1 FAT:

DATE: _____   WATER: 💧💧💧💧💧💧💧💧

MORNING GOALS:

BREAKFAST	LUNCH	DINNER
1 PROTEIN:	1 PROTEIN:	1 PROTEIN:
1 GRAIN:	6OZ VEGETABLE:	6OZ VEGETABLE:
1 FRUIT:	1 FRUIT:	8OZ SALAD:
	1 FAT:	1 FAT:

DATE: _____ WATER: ○ ○ ○ ○ ○ ○ ○ ○

MORNING GOALS:

BREAKFAST

1 PROTEIN:

1 GRAIN:

1 FRUIT:

LUNCH

1 PROTEIN:

6OZ VEGETABLE:

1 FRUIT:

1 FAT:

DINNER

1 PROTEIN:

6OZ VEGETABLE:

8OZ SALAD:

1 FAT:

DATE: _____ WATER: ◯ ◯ ◯ ◯ ◯ ◯ ◯ ◯

MORNING GOALS:

BREAKFAST

1 PROTEIN:

1 GRAIN:

1 FRUIT:

LUNCH

1 PROTEIN:

6OZ VEGETABLE:

1 FRUIT:

1 FAT:

DINNER

1 PROTEIN:

6OZ VEGETABLE:

8OZ SALAD:

1 FAT:

DATE: _____ WATER: ○ ○ ○ ○ ○ ○ ○ ○

MORNING GOALS:

BREAKFAST

1 PROTEIN:

1 GRAIN:

1 FRUIT:

LUNCH

1 PROTEIN:

6OZ VEGETABLE:

1 FRUIT:

1 FAT:

DINNER

1 PROTEIN:

6OZ VEGETABLE:

8OZ SALAD:

1 FAT:

DATE: _____   WATER: ○ ○ ○ ○ ○ ○ ○ ○

MORNING GOALS:

BREAKFAST

1 PROTEIN:

1 GRAIN:

1 FRUIT:

LUNCH

1 PROTEIN:

6OZ VEGETABLE:

1 FRUIT:

1 FAT:

DINNER

1 PROTEIN:

6OZ VEGETABLE:

8OZ SALAD:

1 FAT:

DATE: _____ WATER: ○ ○ ○ ○ ○ ○ ○ ○

MORNING GOALS:

BREAKFAST

1 PROTEIN:

1 GRAIN:

1 FRUIT:

LUNCH

1 PROTEIN:

6OZ VEGETABLE:

1 FRUIT:

1 FAT:

DINNER

1 PROTEIN:

6OZ VEGETABLE:

8OZ SALAD:

1 FAT:

DATE: _____ WATER: ○ ○ ○ ○ ○ ○ ○ ○

MORNING GOALS:

BREAKFAST	LUNCH	DINNER
1 PROTEIN:	1 PROTEIN:	1 PROTEIN:
1 GRAIN:	6OZ VEGETABLE:	6OZ VEGETABLE:
1 FRUIT:	1 FRUIT:	8OZ SALAD:
	1 FAT:	1 FAT:

DATE: _____   WATER: ○ ○ ○ ○ ○ ○ ○ ○

MORNING GOALS:

BREAKFAST

1 PROTEIN:

1 GRAIN:

1 FRUIT:

LUNCH

1 PROTEIN:

6OZ VEGETABLE:

1 FRUIT:

1 FAT:

DINNER

1 PROTEIN:

6OZ VEGETABLE:

8OZ SALAD:

1 FAT:

DATE: _____   WATER: ○ ○ ○ ○ ○ ○ ○ ○

MORNING GOALS:

BREAKFAST	LUNCH	DINNER
1 PROTEIN:	1 PROTEIN:	1 PROTEIN:
1 GRAIN:	6OZ VEGETABLE:	6OZ VEGETABLE:
1 FRUIT:	1 FRUIT:	8OZ SALAD:
	1 FAT:	1 FAT:

DATE: _____   WATER: 💧 💧 💧 💧 💧 💧 💧 💧

MORNING GOALS:

BREAKFAST	LUNCH	DINNER
1 PROTEIN:	1 PROTEIN:	1 PROTEIN:
1 GRAIN:	6OZ VEGETABLE:	6OZ VEGETABLE:
1 FRUIT:	1 FRUIT:	8OZ SALAD:
	1 FAT:	1 FAT:

DATE: _____   WATER: ○ ○ ○ ○ ○ ○ ○ ○

MORNING GOALS:

BREAKFAST	LUNCH	DINNER
1 PROTEIN:	1 PROTEIN:	1 PROTEIN:
1 GRAIN:	6OZ VEGETABLE:	6OZ VEGETABLE:
1 FRUIT:	1 FRUIT:	8OZ SALAD:
	1 FAT:	1 FAT:

DATE: _____   WATER: ○ ○ ○ ○ ○ ○ ○ ○

MORNING GOALS:

BREAKFAST

1 PROTEIN:

1 GRAIN:

1 FRUIT:

LUNCH

1 PROTEIN:

6OZ VEGETABLE:

1 FRUIT:

1 FAT:

DINNER

1 PROTEIN:

6OZ VEGETABLE:

8OZ SALAD:

1 FAT:

DATE: _____ WATER: ○ ○ ○ ○ ○ ○ ○ ○

MORNING GOALS:

BREAKFAST	LUNCH	DINNER
1 PROTEIN:	1 PROTEIN:	1 PROTEIN:
1 GRAIN:	6OZ VEGETABLE:	6OZ VEGETABLE:
1 FRUIT:	1 FRUIT:	8OZ SALAD:
	1 FAT:	1 FAT:

DATE: _____   WATER: ⬯ ⬯ ⬯ ⬯ ⬯ ⬯ ⬯ ⬯

MORNING GOALS:

BREAKFAST

1 PROTEIN:

1 GRAIN:

1 FRUIT:

LUNCH

1 PROTEIN:

6OZ VEGETABLE:

1 FRUIT:

1 FAT:

DINNER

1 PROTEIN:

6OZ VEGETABLE:

8OZ SALAD:

1 FAT:

DATE: _____   WATER: 💧💧💧💧💧💧💧💧

MORNING GOALS:

BREAKFAST	LUNCH	DINNER
1 PROTEIN:	1 PROTEIN:	1 PROTEIN:
1 GRAIN:	6OZ VEGETABLE:	6OZ VEGETABLE:
1 FRUIT:	1 FRUIT:	8OZ SALAD:
	1 FAT:	1 FAT:

DATE: _____ WATER: ◯ ◯ ◯ ◯ ◯ ◯ ◯ ◯

MORNING GOALS:

BREAKFAST

1 PROTEIN:

1 GRAIN:

1 FRUIT:

LUNCH

1 PROTEIN:

6OZ VEGETABLE:

1 FRUIT:

1 FAT:

DINNER

1 PROTEIN:

6OZ VEGETABLE:

8OZ SALAD:

1 FAT:

DATE: _____   WATER: 💧💧💧💧💧💧💧

MORNING GOALS:

BREAKFAST	LUNCH	DINNER
1 PROTEIN:	1 PROTEIN:	1 PROTEIN:
1 GRAIN:	6OZ VEGETABLE:	6OZ VEGETABLE:
1 FRUIT:	1 FRUIT:	8OZ SALAD:
	1 FAT:	1 FAT:

DATE: _____ WATER: ○ ○ ○ ○ ○ ○ ○ ○

MORNING GOALS:

BREAKFAST

1 PROTEIN:

1 GRAIN:

1 FRUIT:

LUNCH

1 PROTEIN:

6OZ VEGETABLE:

1 FRUIT:

1 FAT:

DINNER

1 PROTEIN:

6OZ VEGETABLE:

8OZ SALAD:

1 FAT:

DATE: _____   WATER: ◊ ◊ ◊ ◊ ◊ ◊ ◊ ◊

MORNING GOALS:

BREAKFAST	LUNCH	DINNER
1 PROTEIN:	1 PROTEIN:	1 PROTEIN:
1 GRAIN:	6OZ VEGETABLE:	6OZ VEGETABLE:
1 FRUIT:	1 FRUIT:	8OZ SALAD:
	1 FAT:	1 FAT:

DATE: _____   WATER: ○ ○ ○ ○ ○ ○ ○ ○

MORNING GOALS:

BREAKFAST

1 PROTEIN:

1 GRAIN:

1 FRUIT:

LUNCH

1 PROTEIN:

6OZ VEGETABLE:

1 FRUIT:

1 FAT:

DINNER

1 PROTEIN:

6OZ VEGETABLE:

8OZ SALAD:

1 FAT:

DATE: _____ WATER: ⬦ ⬦ ⬦ ⬦ ⬦ ⬦ ⬦

MORNING GOALS:

BREAKFAST	LUNCH	DINNER
1 PROTEIN:	1 PROTEIN:	1 PROTEIN:
1 GRAIN:	6OZ VEGETABLE:	6OZ VEGETABLE:
1 FRUIT:	1 FRUIT:	8OZ SALAD:
	1 FAT:	1 FAT:

DATE: _____   WATER: ◯ ◯ ◯ ◯ ◯ ◯ ◯ ◯

MORNING GOALS:

BREAKFAST	LUNCH	DINNER
1 PROTEIN:	1 PROTEIN:	1 PROTEIN:
1 GRAIN:	6OZ VEGETABLE:	6OZ VEGETABLE:
1 FRUIT:	1 FRUIT:	8OZ SALAD:
	1 FAT:	1 FAT:

DATE: _____   WATER: ⚪ ⚪ ⚪ ⚪ ⚪ ⚪ ⚪ ⚪

MORNING GOALS:

BREAKFAST	LUNCH	DINNER
1 PROTEIN:	1 PROTEIN:	1 PROTEIN:
1 GRAIN:	6OZ VEGETABLE:	6OZ VEGETABLE:
1 FRUIT:	1 FRUIT:	8OZ SALAD:
	1 FAT:	1 FAT:

DATE: _____   WATER: ◊ ◊ ◊ ◊ ◊ ◊ ◊ ◊

MORNING GOALS:

BREAKFAST

1 PROTEIN:

1 GRAIN:

1 FRUIT:

LUNCH

1 PROTEIN:

6OZ VEGETABLE:

1 FRUIT:

1 FAT:

DINNER

1 PROTEIN:

6OZ VEGETABLE:

8OZ SALAD:

1 FAT:

DATE: _____   WATER: 💧💧💧💧💧💧💧💧

MORNING GOALS:

BREAKFAST

1 PROTEIN:

1 GRAIN:

1 FRUIT:

LUNCH

1 PROTEIN:

6OZ VEGETABLE:

1 FRUIT:

1 FAT:

DINNER

1 PROTEIN:

6OZ VEGETABLE:

8OZ SALAD:

1 FAT:

DATE: _____   WATER: 💧💧💧💧💧💧💧💧

MORNING GOALS:

BREAKFAST

1 PROTEIN:

1 GRAIN:

1 FRUIT:

LUNCH

1 PROTEIN:

6OZ VEGETABLE:

1 FRUIT:

1 FAT:

DINNER

1 PROTEIN:

6OZ VEGETABLE:

8OZ SALAD:

1 FAT:

DATE: _____   WATER: ○ ○ ○ ○ ○ ○ ○ ○

MORNING GOALS:

BREAKFAST	LUNCH	DINNER
1 PROTEIN:	1 PROTEIN:	1 PROTEIN:
1 GRAIN:	6OZ VEGETABLE:	6OZ VEGETABLE:
1 FRUIT:	1 FRUIT:	8OZ SALAD:
	1 FAT:	1 FAT:

DATE: _____   WATER: ⬭ ⬭ ⬭ ⬭ ⬭ ⬭ ⬭ ⬭

MORNING GOALS:

BREAKFAST	LUNCH	DINNER
1 PROTEIN:	1 PROTEIN:	1 PROTEIN:
1 GRAIN:	6OZ VEGETABLE:	6OZ VEGETABLE:
1 FRUIT:	1 FRUIT:	8OZ SALAD:
	1 FAT:	1 FAT:

DATE: _____   WATER: 💧 💧 💧 💧 💧 💧 💧 💧

MORNING GOALS:

BREAKFAST	LUNCH	DINNER
1 PROTEIN:	1 PROTEIN:	1 PROTEIN:
1 GRAIN:	6OZ VEGETABLE:	6OZ VEGETABLE:
1 FRUIT:	1 FRUIT:	8OZ SALAD:
	1 FAT:	1 FAT:

DATE: _____ WATER: ⬡ ⬡ ⬡ ⬡ ⬡ ⬡ ⬡ ⬡

MORNING GOALS:

BREAKFAST

1 PROTEIN:

1 GRAIN:

1 FRUIT:

LUNCH

1 PROTEIN:

6OZ VEGETABLE:

1 FRUIT:

1 FAT:

DINNER

1 PROTEIN:

6OZ VEGETABLE:

8OZ SALAD:

1 FAT:

DATE: _____   WATER: ⚪ ⚪ ⚪ ⚪ ⚪ ⚪ ⚪ ⚪

MORNING GOALS:

BREAKFAST	LUNCH	DINNER
1 PROTEIN:	1 PROTEIN:	1 PROTEIN:
1 GRAIN:	6OZ VEGETABLE:	6OZ VEGETABLE:
1 FRUIT:	1 FRUIT:	8OZ SALAD:
	1 FAT:	1 FAT:

DATE: _____ WATER: ◇ ◇ ◇ ◇ ◇ ◇ ◇ ◇

MORNING GOALS:

BREAKFAST

1 PROTEIN:

1 GRAIN:

1 FRUIT:

LUNCH

1 PROTEIN:

6OZ VEGETABLE:

1 FRUIT:

1 FAT:

DINNER

1 PROTEIN:

6OZ VEGETABLE:

8OZ SALAD:

1 FAT:

DATE: _____ WATER: ⬭ ⬭ ⬭ ⬭ ⬭ ⬭ ⬭ ⬭

MORNING GOALS:

BREAKFAST	LUNCH	DINNER
1 PROTEIN:	1 PROTEIN:	1 PROTEIN:
1 GRAIN:	6OZ VEGETABLE:	6OZ VEGETABLE:
1 FRUIT:	1 FRUIT:	8OZ SALAD:
	1 FAT:	1 FAT:

DATE: _____   WATER: 💧💧💧💧💧💧💧

MORNING GOALS:

BREAKFAST	LUNCH	DINNER
1 PROTEIN:	1 PROTEIN:	1 PROTEIN:
1 GRAIN:	6OZ VEGETABLE:	6OZ VEGETABLE:
1 FRUIT:	1 FRUIT:	8OZ SALAD:
	1 FAT:	1 FAT:

DATE: _____   WATER: ○ ○ ○ ○ ○ ○ ○ ○

MORNING GOALS:

BREAKFAST

1 PROTEIN:

1 GRAIN:

1 FRUIT:

LUNCH

1 PROTEIN:

6OZ VEGETABLE:

1 FRUIT:

1 FAT:

DINNER

1 PROTEIN:

6OZ VEGETABLE:

8OZ SALAD:

1 FAT:

DATE: _____   WATER: ○ ○ ○ ○ ○ ○ ○ ○

MORNING GOALS:

BREAKFAST

1 PROTEIN:

1 GRAIN:

1 FRUIT:

LUNCH

1 PROTEIN:

6OZ VEGETABLE:

1 FRUIT:

1 FAT:

DINNER

1 PROTEIN:

6OZ VEGETABLE:

8OZ SALAD:

1 FAT:

DATE: _____   WATER: ○ ○ ○ ○ ○ ○ ○

MORNING GOALS:

BREAKFAST	LUNCH	DINNER
1 PROTEIN:	1 PROTEIN:	1 PROTEIN:
1 GRAIN:	6OZ VEGETABLE:	6OZ VEGETABLE:
1 FRUIT:	1 FRUIT:	8OZ SALAD:
	1 FAT:	1 FAT:

DATE: _____ WATER: ⬡ ⬡ ⬡ ⬡ ⬡ ⬡ ⬡ ⬡

MORNING GOALS:

BREAKFAST	LUNCH	DINNER
1 PROTEIN:	1 PROTEIN:	1 PROTEIN:
1 GRAIN:	6OZ VEGETABLE:	6OZ VEGETABLE:
1 FRUIT:	1 FRUIT:	8OZ SALAD:
	1 FAT:	1 FAT:

DATE: _____ WATER: ○ ○ ○ ○ ○ ○ ○ ○

MORNING GOALS:

BREAKFAST

1 PROTEIN:

1 GRAIN:

1 FRUIT:

LUNCH

1 PROTEIN:

6OZ VEGETABLE:

1 FRUIT:

1 FAT:

DINNER

1 PROTEIN:

6OZ VEGETABLE:

8OZ SALAD:

1 FAT:

DATE: _____ WATER: ○ ○ ○ ○ ○ ○ ○ ○

MORNING GOALS:

BREAKFAST

1 PROTEIN:

1 GRAIN:

1 FRUIT:

LUNCH

1 PROTEIN:

6OZ VEGETABLE:

1 FRUIT:

1 FAT:

DINNER

1 PROTEIN:

6OZ VEGETABLE:

8OZ SALAD:

1 FAT:

DATE: _____   WATER: ○ ○ ○ ○ ○ ○ ○ ○

MORNING GOALS:

BREAKFAST

1 PROTEIN:

1 GRAIN:

1 FRUIT:

LUNCH

1 PROTEIN:

6OZ VEGETABLE:

1 FRUIT:

1 FAT:

DINNER

1 PROTEIN:

6OZ VEGETABLE:

8OZ SALAD:

1 FAT:

DATE: _____ WATER: ○ ○ ○ ○ ○ ○ ○ ○

MORNING GOALS:

BREAKFAST

1 PROTEIN:

1 GRAIN:

1 FRUIT:

LUNCH

1 PROTEIN:

6OZ VEGETABLE:

1 FRUIT:

1 FAT:

DINNER

1 PROTEIN:

6OZ VEGETABLE:

8OZ SALAD:

1 FAT:

DATE: _____   WATER: 💧💧💧💧💧💧💧💧

MORNING GOALS:

BREAKFAST

1 PROTEIN:

1 GRAIN:

1 FRUIT:

LUNCH

1 PROTEIN:

6OZ VEGETABLE:

1 FRUIT:

1 FAT:

DINNER

1 PROTEIN:

6OZ VEGETABLE:

8OZ SALAD:

1 FAT:

DATE: _____ WATER: ◊ ◊ ◊ ◊ ◊ ◊ ◊ ◊

MORNING GOALS:

BREAKFAST	LUNCH	DINNER
1 PROTEIN:	1 PROTEIN:	1 PROTEIN:
1 GRAIN:	6OZ VEGETABLE:	6OZ VEGETABLE:
1 FRUIT:	1 FRUIT:	8OZ SALAD:
	1 FAT:	1 FAT:

DATE: _____   WATER: 💧 💧 💧 💧 💧 💧 💧 💧

MORNING GOALS:

BREAKFAST

1 PROTEIN:

1 GRAIN:

1 FRUIT:

LUNCH

1 PROTEIN:

6OZ VEGETABLE:

1 FRUIT:

1 FAT:

DINNER

1 PROTEIN:

6OZ VEGETABLE:

8OZ SALAD:

1 FAT:

DATE: _____   WATER: ○ ○ ○ ○ ○ ○ ○ ○

MORNING GOALS:

BREAKFAST	LUNCH	DINNER
1 PROTEIN:	1 PROTEIN:	1 PROTEIN:
1 GRAIN:	6OZ VEGETABLE:	6OZ VEGETABLE:
1 FRUIT:	1 FRUIT:	8OZ SALAD:
	1 FAT:	1 FAT:

DATE: _____

WATER: ◯ ◯ ◯ ◯ ◯ ◯ ◯ ◯

MORNING GOALS:

BREAKFAST

1 PROTEIN:

1 GRAIN:

1 FRUIT:

LUNCH

1 PROTEIN:

6OZ VEGETABLE:

1 FRUIT:

1 FAT:

DINNER

1 PROTEIN:

6OZ VEGETABLE:

8OZ SALAD:

1 FAT:

DATE: _____ WATER: 💧 💧 💧 💧 💧 💧 💧 💧

MORNING GOALS:

BREAKFAST

1 PROTEIN:

1 GRAIN:

1 FRUIT:

LUNCH

1 PROTEIN:

6OZ VEGETABLE:

1 FRUIT:

1 FAT:

DINNER

1 PROTEIN:

6OZ VEGETABLE:

8OZ SALAD:

1 FAT:

DATE: _____   WATER: ○ ○ ○ ○ ○ ○ ○ ○

MORNING GOALS:

BREAKFAST

1 PROTEIN:

1 GRAIN:

1 FRUIT:

LUNCH

1 PROTEIN:

6OZ VEGETABLE:

1 FRUIT:

1 FAT:

DINNER

1 PROTEIN:

6OZ VEGETABLE:

8OZ SALAD:

1 FAT:

DATE: _____ WATER: ○ ○ ○ ○ ○ ○ ○ ○

MORNING GOALS:

BREAKFAST

1 PROTEIN:

1 GRAIN:

1 FRUIT:

LUNCH

1 PROTEIN:

6OZ VEGETABLE:

1 FRUIT:

1 FAT:

DINNER

1 PROTEIN:

6OZ VEGETABLE:

8OZ SALAD:

1 FAT:

Made in the
USA
Monee, IL